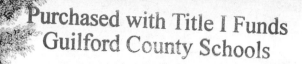

DISCOVER
The Thirteen Colonies

by Barbara Brannon

Table of Contents

T3074

Introduction

Many **colonists** came on ships.
Many colonists came to thirteen **colonies**.

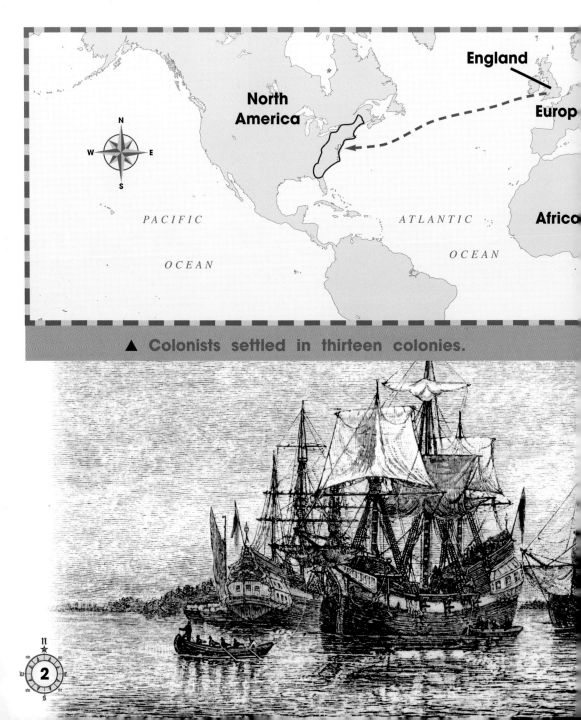

North America

England

Europ

Africa

PACIFIC OCEAN

ATLANTIC OCEAN

▲ Colonists settled in thirteen colonies.

Words to Know

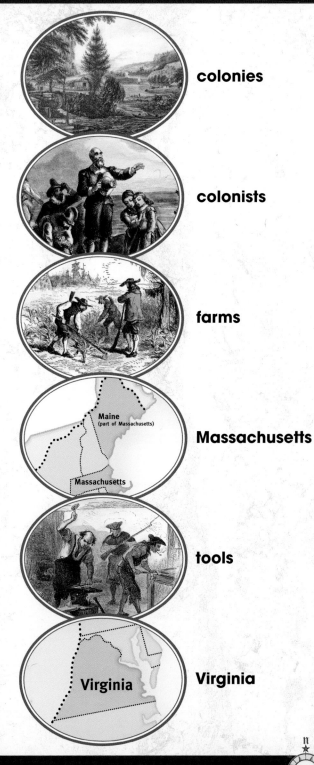

colonies

colonists

farms

Massachusetts

Maine
(part of Massachusetts)

Massachusetts

tools

Virginia

Virginia

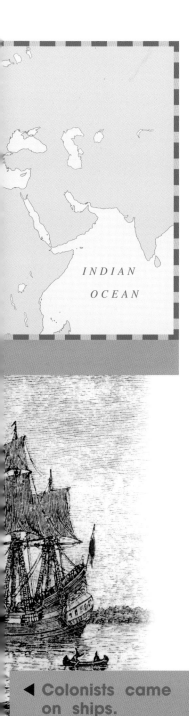

INDIAN
OCEAN

Where Did the Colonists Go?

Many colonists went to **Virginia**. Many colonists went to live there.

▲ Colonists went to Jamestown, Virginia.

Many colonists went to **Massachusetts**. Many colonists went to live there.

▲ Colonists went to Plymouth, Massachusetts.

What Was Life Like for the Colonists?

The colonists had **farms**.

▲ Colonists had farms.

The colonists had **tools**.

▲ Colonists had tools.

What Did the Colonists Build?

The colonists built houses.

Colonists had ▶
houses.

The colonists built schools.

◀ Colonists had
schools.

The colonists built buildings.

▲ Colonists had buildings.

Chapter 3

The colonists built roads.

▲ The colonists had roads.

The colonists built boats.

▲ Colonists had boats.

Conclusion

The colonists built colonies.

Concept Map

The Thirteen Colonies

Where Did the Colonists Go?

Virginia

Massachusetts

other colonies

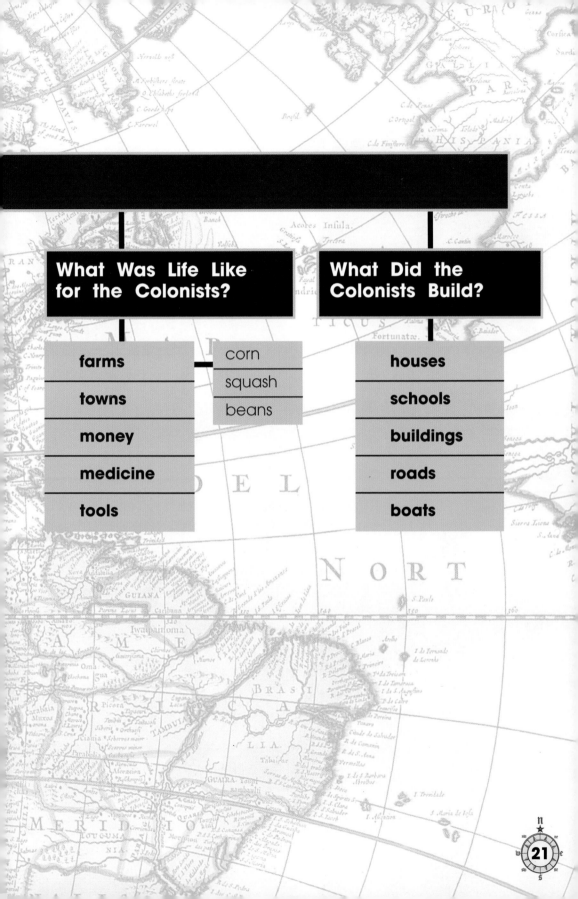

What Was Life Like for the Colonists?		**What Did the Colonists Build?**	
farms	corn	**houses**	
towns	squash	**schools**	
money	beans	**buildings**	
medicine		**roads**	
tools		**boats**	

Glossary

colonies settlements ruled by another country

*Many colonists went to thirteen **colonies**.*

colonists people who lived in the colonies

*Many **colonists** went to Virginia.*

farms places where people live and grow crops

*The colonists had **farms**.*

Maine
(part of Massachusetts)

Massachusetts

Massachusetts one of the thirteen colonies

*Many colonists went to **Massachusetts**.*

tools objects used to do work

*The colonists had **tools**.*

Virginia

Virginia one of the thirteen colonies

*Many colonists went to **Virginia**.*

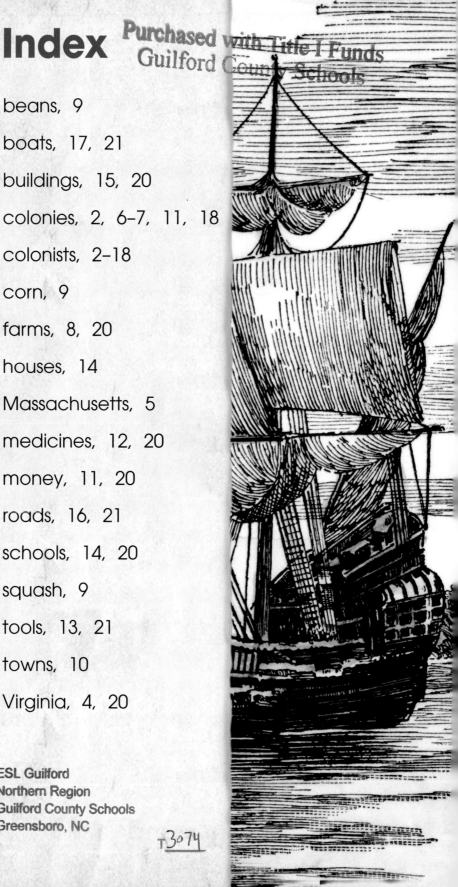

Index

T3074